JOURNAL
WHAT GOD HAS FOR ME IS MINE

My Name Is on It

By Dr. Tonia Ann Walker

DEDICATION PAGE

This Journal is for every daughter of God who has walked through seasons of breaking, birthing, and becoming. To every student I have taught, every woman I have prayed for, and every soul God has assigned to my voice, for those who believed in me before I believed in myself.

Dr. Tonia Ann Walker

"I am coaching, motivating, and educating others through my lived experiences."

COPYRIGHT PAGE

TABLE OF CONTENTS

INTRODUCTION

What God Has for Me Is Mine: *"My Name Is on It"* is more than a journal, it is a declaration of faith, purpose, and divine alignment.

It is a reminder that no matter what you have faced, what doors have closed, or how long the wait has been, *what belongs to you cannot be lost.*

This journal was created to walk alongside you as you grow, heal, and move boldly into everything God has promised. Each section reflects a stage of the journey, shifting, releasing, resting, and rising again. As you write, allow your spirit to speak freely. There is no right or wrong way to show up on these pages. Some days you may write paragraphs; other days, a single line may carry the weight of your soul.

Let this be a sacred space, between you and God, where revelation meets reflection, and healing turns into forward movement. You have already come so far. Now it is time to move *into* what is next... fully, freely, and faithfully.

With love and purpose,

Dr. Tonia Ann Walker

How to Use This Journal

This journal is designed to help you reflect, pray, and record your spiritual growth as you move through life's seasons with purpose. Here is how to get the most out of it:

1. **Prepare Your Heart** – Begin each session with quiet time, prayer, or scripture reading. Ask God to reveal what He wants you to see in that moment.

2. **Read the Reflection Title** – Let each chapter heading speak to where you are. The titles follow natural progression, from finding purpose to letting go and moving forward.

3. **Answer the Prompts Honestly** – Do not hold back. Write your truth. God meets you in authenticity.

4. **Include Scripture or Affirmations** – Feel free to write verses or words that strengthen your spirit.

5. **Pause and Revisit** – Some sections may call for more time. It is okay to rest and come back when you are ready.

6. **Celebrate Progress** – Look back on earlier pages from time to time. You will see growth, healing, and prayers written between the lines.

Each page is an opportunity to claim the promises of God and reaffirm:

What God Has for Me is Mine. *"My Name Is on It."*

Dr. Tonia Ann Walker

SECTION ONE
MOVING INTO PURPOSE

Reflection

There comes a moment when you can no longer ignore what God placed inside of you. The pull becomes stronger than the fear, and the desire to stay comfortable fades in comparison to the call on your life. Moving into purpose is not about having all the answers, it is about trusting that God already does.

Purpose does not shout; it whispers. It calls you in the quiet moments, through your passions, your pain, and even your detours. Every experience, good or bad, was preparing you for this moment. You have carried potential long enough. Now, it is time to *walk in it*.

As you move forward, remember purpose is not about perfection. It is about alignment. It is about showing up, one obedient step at a time, knowing that the One who began a good work in you will finish it.

Scripture Meditation

"For I know the plans I have for you," declares the Lord, "plans to prosper you and not to harm you, plans to give you hope and a future."
— Jeremiah 29:11 (NIV)

Affirmation

"I was created with purpose, chosen with intention, and positioned with power. I walk boldly into what God has designed for me."

Prayer Space

Father, thank You for revealing purpose in my life. Even when I can't see the full picture, help me trust you're timing. Give me the courage to take each step with faith, and to know that everything you have placed within me will bloom in its appointed season.
In Jesus' name, Amen.

Reflective Manifestation

1. What does *purpose* mean to me in this season of my life?

Your thoughts:

2. Where have I seen God redirect my path toward something greater?

Your thoughts:

3. What fears or distractions have held me back from moving forward?

Your thoughts:

____

____

____

____

____

____

4. Write about one area where you feel God is calling you to act or step out in faith.

Your thoughts:

____

____

____

____

____

____

SECTION TWO
SHIFTING WITHIN

Reflection

True transformation does not always happen in public. It begins quietly, deep within the heart. Before God changes your surroundings, He often starts by changing *you*.

The shift within is where healing begins, where old patterns are broken, and where your mindset starts to align with His promises. Sometimes it feels uncomfortable, even painful, because the process of growth requires release. But do not resist, embrace it. What God is doing inside of you now will soon show on the outside.

When you begin to think differently, you live differently. When your spirit is renewed, your path becomes clearer. This is your inner shift, your preparation season. Trust that the change within is leading you to everything He has promised you.

Scripture Meditation

"Do not conform to the pattern of this world but be transformed by the renewing of your mind. Then you will be able to test and approve what God's will is, His good, pleasing, and perfect will." — Romans 12:2 (NIV).

Affirmation

"I welcome divine transformation. My heart, mind, and my spirit are renewed daily. I am shifting into alignment with God's perfect will."

Prayer Space

Heavenly Father, thank You for working in me, even when I can't see it. Help me to trust the process and release the parts of me that no longer reflect who You've called me to be. Renew my thoughts, heal my heart, and strengthen my faith as I shift into Your will.
Amen.

Reflective Manifestation

1. What area of my life is God inviting me to shift or surrender?

Your thoughts:

2. How have I felt His hand guiding me to think, act, or speak differently?

Your thoughts:

3. What old habits, fears, or beliefs no longer serve where
    you are going?

Your thoughts:

4. What would my life look like if I fully embraced this
    inner transformation?

Your thoughts:

SECTION THREE
REAPING BLESSINGS FROM THE BATTLE

Reflection

Every battle has a purpose. What you went through was not meant to break you, it was designed to build you. The struggle sharpened your faith, deepened your dependence on God, and prepared you for the blessings that follow.

It is easy to see the pain but look again, you'll find evidence of God's hand in the middle of your trials. The tears you cried watered the soil of your breakthrough. The strength you gained in the storm is the same strength that will carry you into your next season.

Sometimes, blessings do not look like new things; they look like *new perspectives*. When you learn to thank God even for the hard places, you discover that nothing was wasted. Your battle became your birthing ground for blessing.

Scripture Meditation

"And we know that in all things God works for the good of those who love Him, who have been called according to His purpose."
— Romans 8:28 (NIV)

Affirmation

"Every battle I have faced has birthed a blessing. My scars tell the story of survival, strength, and God's unshakable faithfulness."

Prayer Space

Father, thank You for turning my pain into purpose. Help me to see the beauty in every battle and to trust that You were with me all along. May I never forget that even in the fight, I was being formed for greater. Let my victories glorify You and remind me that blessings often bloom from broken places. Amen.

Reflective Manifestation

1. What recent battle has tested your faith the most?

Your thoughts:

2. What lessons or strengths have I gained from that experience?

Your thoughts:

3. How has God shown Himself faithful, even when you
    could not see the full picture?

Your thoughts:

4. In what ways can I now use what I have learned to
    encourage someone else?

Your thoughts:

SECTION FOUR
IDENTIFYING MY POWER

Power is not loud or flashy. True power is quiet, steady, and rooted in who God created you to be. It lives in your convictions, your faith, and your ability to persevere despite circumstances.

Often, we overlook our own strength because we measure it against someone else's. But your power is uniquely yours, shaped by your experiences, refined through trials, and illuminated by God's presence in your life.

Take time to recognize it. Celebrate it. Write it down. The more you identify your God-given power, the more confidently you can step into your purpose, face challenges, and walk boldly toward your calling.

Scripture Meditation

"I can do all this through Him who gives me strength."
— Philippians 4:13 (NIV)

Affirmation

"I am powerful because God's Spirit lives in me. My strength, wisdom, and gifts are perfectly designed for the calling He has placed on my life."

Prayer Space

Heavenly Father, thank You for the power You've placed inside me. Help me recognize it, embrace it, and use it for Your glory. Give me boldness to step into my calling with confidence, knowing You equip me for every task.
Amen.

Reflective Manifestation

1. What are three strengths God has given me that I often overlook?

Your thoughts:

2. How has my faith carried me through challenges in ways I did not realize?

Your thoughts:

3. Where have I relied on my own power instead of God's?
    How did that turn out?

Your thoughts:

4. How can I intentionally use my gifts and strengths to
    bless others?

Your thoughts:

SECTION FIVE
REMOVING COMPARISONS

Reflection

Comparison is a thief of joy. When you measure your journey against someone else's, you miss the unique path God has designed for you. Your story, your timing, and your gifts are unlike anyone else's, and that's exactly how God intended it.

Let go of the urge to compete, to measure, or to wish for someone else's life. Your progress, your victories, and even your struggles are meant to shape *your* purpose, not anyone else's. Embrace your journey with gratitude and watch how freedom replaces fear when comparison no longer holds power over you.

Scripture Meditation

"For we are God's handiwork, created in Christ Jesus to do good works, which God prepared in advance for us to do."
— Ephesians 2:10 (NIV)

Affirmation

"God uniquely creates me. My path is mine alone, and I release all comparisons that steal my joy and purpose."

Prayer Space

Lord, help me to see myself through Your eyes, not the world's. Remove the habit of comparison and remind me that Your plan for me is perfect. Teach me to celebrate my journey and the gifts You have given me, trusting that my timing and purpose are divine.
Amen.

Reflective Manifestation

1. In what areas of life do I tend to compare myself to others?

Your thoughts:

2. How has comparison held me back or caused unnecessary worry?

Your thoughts:

3. What blessings, talents, or experiences are uniquely
    mine?

Your thoughts:

4. Write down three affirmations of self-worth rooted in
    God's truth.

Your thoughts:

SECTION SIX
DANCING AT THE CLOSED DOOR

Reflection

Sometimes God closes a door, and it feels like rejection. But closed doors are often divine protection, steering us away from what is not meant for us and toward what is.

Dancing at the closed door is about celebrating even when things do not go as planned. It is learning to trust God's timing and rejoice in His wisdom. Every "no" is a redirection, a pause that preserves your peace and prepares you for the next season.

Instead of feeling disappointed, I find freedom in gratitude. Celebrate what you *have* instead of what you *do not*. The closed doors of today are often the gateways to the blessings of tomorrow.

Scripture Meditation

"Trust in the Lord with all your heart and lean not on your own understanding; in all your ways submit to Him, and He will make your paths straight."
— Proverbs 3:5-6 (NIV)

Affirmation

"I celebrate God's timing and trust His plan. Closed doors are not the end, but a pathway to greater blessings."

Prayer Space

Father, thank You for guiding me even when I cannot see the full picture. Help me to trust Your plan, rejoice in Your protection, and embrace the doors You open in Your perfect timing.
Amen.

Reflective Manifestation

1. What doors have closed in my life recently, and how did I respond?

Your thoughts:

2. How can I celebrate God's protection in situations that did not go as planned?

Your thoughts:

3. What lessons have I learned from setbacks or disappointments?

Your thoughts:

4. Write down one area where God is redirecting you toward something better.

Your thoughts:

SECTION SEVEN
WAITING FOR CONFIRMATION FROM GOD

Reflection

Waiting is never easy, but it is powerful. God often calls us to pause, to prepare, and to trust Him fully before moving forward. Waiting for confirmation is not about hesitation, it is about alignment.

When we rush ahead, we risk missing the blessings that come with His timing. But when we wait with faith, we allow God to show us His plan clearly. Patience strengthens trust, builds character, and refines our hearts.

Use this season of waiting to listen, pray, and discern. God speaks in whispers, nudges, and quiet confirmations. The more you tune in, the easier it is to recognize His voice when He says, "This is the way. Walk in it."

Scripture Meditation

"Be still before the Lord and wait patiently for Him;
do not fret when people succeed in their ways, when they carry
out their wicked schemes."
— Psalm 37:7 (NIV)

Affirmation

"I wait with faith, trusting that God's timing is perfect. I am confident that His guidance will lead me to the right path."

Prayer Space

Heavenly Father, thank You for Your perfect timing. Help me to trust You fully as I wait for Your confirmation. Give me patience, peace, and discernment, so I may recognize Your voice clearly and step boldly when You say, 'Go.'
Amen.

Reflective Manifestation

1. What am I waiting for from God right now?

Your thoughts:

2. How have I experienced His timing in past situations?

Your thoughts:

3. What can I do to remain patient and faithful during this waiting period?

Your thoughts:

4. Write down any "signs" or confirmations you feel God is giving you.

Your thoughts:

SECTION EIGHT
REMOVING LABELS

Reflection

Labels can limit us more than any obstacle. Sometimes, they come from other words that were spoken over us in childhood, in school, or even in adulthood. Other times, they are self-imposed, the negative beliefs we have accepted as truth.

God sees you differently. He does not define you by your past mistakes, failures, or what anyone else thinks of you. You are His masterpiece, created with purpose, love, and intention. Removing labels is about reclaiming your identity and stepping into freedom.

Let go of names that do not belong to you, and embrace the truth: you are chosen, beloved, and empowered to fulfill your divine purpose.

Scripture Meditation

"So, God created mankind in His own image, in the image of God He created them; male and female He created them."— Genesis 1:27 (NIV)

Affirmation

"I am defined by God, not by the opinions or expectations of others. I release all labels that limit my purpose and embrace my identity in Him."

Prayer Space

Father, thank You for creating me in Your image and defining my worth. Help me to reject the labels that don't belong to me and to walk confidently in the identity You have given me. May Your truth guide my thoughts, words, and actions every day. Amen.

Reflective Manifestation

1. What negative labels have I accepted about myself?

Your thoughts:

2. Where did these labels originate, and are they true?

Your thoughts:

3. How does God see me differently than the world sees
    me?

Your thoughts:

4. Write down the positive, God-given truths about yourself
    that replace these labels.

Your thoughts:

SECTION NINE
TAKING REST BEFORE THE NEXT

Reflection

Rest is not a sign of weakness; it is a sacred part of the journey. Before stepping into the next season, God often calls us to pause, recharge, and reflect. Taking rest allows your mind, body, and spirit to align with His will.

Many of us rush from one task to another, believing productivity equals progress. But true progress comes when we honor God's rhythm, resting, reflecting, and preparing for what's next. During rest, God renews your strength, sharpens your vision, and restores your heart.

Give yourself permission to pause. Celebrate the season you are leaving behind and prepare your heart for the blessings ahead.

Scripture Meditation

"Come to me, all you who are weary and burdened, and I will give you rest. Take my yoke upon you and learn from me, for I am gentle and humble in heart, and you will find rest for your souls."— Matthew 11:28-29 (NIV)

Affirmation

"I allow myself to rest in God's timing. My pause is purposeful, and I am renewed for the next season of my life."

Prayer Space

Heavenly Father, thank You for the gift of rest. Help me to pause without guilt, reflect on my journey, and prepare my heart for what You have next. Renew my strength, refresh my spirit, and guide me into the next season with clarity and peace. Amen.

Reflective Manifestation

1. In what areas of life do I need rest right now?

Your thoughts:

2. How can I intentionally pause to recharge spiritually, mentally, and physically?

Your thoughts:

3. What lessons or victories from my current season should
    I reflect on before moving forward?

Your thoughts:

4. Write down one way I can prepare my heart and mind
    for the next chapter.

Your thoughts:

SECTION TEN
LETTING GO OF THE PAST

Reflection

The past can be heavy if we carry it with us. Regret, pain, and past mistakes can weigh down your spirit and block the path God has for you. Letting go is not forgetting it is releasing what no longer serves you and trusting God to redeem every experience.

God wants you to move forward unburdened. Every lesson, every heartbreak, every triumph has led you to this moment. By letting go, you create space for new blessings, opportunities, and growth. Remember, holding on to yesterday keeps you from fully embracing today.

Release, forgive, and step into freedom. Your story is not over, this is the turning point toward purpose, joy, and divine fulfillment.

Scripture Meditation

"Forget the former things; do not dwell on the past.
See, I am doing a new thing! Now it springs up; do you not perceive it? I am making a way in the wilderness and streams in the wasteland."
— Isaiah 43:18-19 (NIV)

Affirmation

"I release the past into God's hands. I walk forward in freedom, trusting His plan and embracing the new things He is doing in my life."

Prayer Space

Father, thank You for Your grace and redemption. Help me to release my past and all the burdens I've carried. Teach me to forgive, to heal, and to step boldly into the new season You have prepared for me.
Amen.

Reflective Manifestation

1. What parts of my past am I holding onto that hinder my progress?

Your thoughts:

2. How has God already used past experiences to prepare me for today?

Your thoughts:

3. What forgiveness of myself or others do I need to extend
    to release the past?

Your thoughts:

4. Write a declaration of freedom, letting go of what no
    longer serves you.

Your thoughts:

SECTION ELEVEN
BEING OBEDIENT TO GOD

Reflection

Obedience is the bridge between faith and fulfillment. It is not always easy, and it does not always make sense in the moment. Yet, when we obey God, we position ourselves to receive His blessings, guidance, and protection.

Obedience is more than following rules, it is a heart posture. It is saying *yes* to God even when it's uncomfortable, inconvenient, or unknown. Each act of obedience strengthens your faith, refines your character, and aligns you with His purpose.

Remember, obedience is not about perfection. It is about a willing heart that seeks God first, trusts His timing, and acts when He calls.

Scripture Meditation

"But Samuel replied: 'Does the Lord delight in burnt offerings and sacrifices as much as in obeying the Lord? To obey is better than sacrifice, and to heed is better than the fat of rams.'"
— 1 Samuel 15:22 (NIV)

Affirmation

"I choose obedience over convenience. I trust God's plan and walk faithfully in the steps He has laid before me."

Prayer Space

Heavenly Father, thank You for Your guidance and wisdom. Help me to obey You wholeheartedly, trusting that Your ways are higher than mine. Give me courage, clarity, and faith to take the steps You have called me to walk, and let my obedience bring glory to Your name.
Amen.

Reflective Manifestation

1. In what areas of my life has God asked me to be obedient?

Your thoughts:

2. How have I experienced blessings when I followed His guidance?

Your thoughts:

3. What fears or hesitations keep me from obeying
   fully?

Your thoughts:

4. Write one action step I can take this week to follow God's
   direction faithfully.

Your thoughts:

SECTION TWELVE
ACCEPTING BEAUTY FOR ASHES

Reflection

Life sometimes brings trials that leave us feeling broken, hurt, or diminished. Yet God promises to bring beauty from what seems lost. The ashes of disappointment, pain, or loss are never the end, they are the soil from which new blessings and purpose emerge.

Accepting beauty for ashes requires faith. It requires trust that God sees the full picture when we only see fragments. It means believing that He can transform heartbreak into hope, sorrow into joy, and failure into favor.

When you embrace His restoration, your past becomes a testimony, your pain becomes a platform, and your life becomes a living proof of His grace.

Scripture Meditation

"I will give you a new heart and put a new spirit in you; I will remove from you your heart of stone and give you a heart of flesh. I will put My Spirit in you and move you to follow My decrees and be careful to keep My laws."
— Ezekiel 36:26-27 (NIV)

Affirmation

"I accept God's transformation in my life. He makes all things new, turning my ashes into beauty and my sorrow into joy."

Prayer Space

Heavenly Father, thank You for Your power to restore and renew. Help me to accept Your beauty in place of my ashes and trust Your plan for my life. Let my heart remain open to Your transformation, and may my life reflect Your glory in every season.
Amen.

Reflective Manifestation

1. What painful experiences have I carried that need God's restoration?

Your thoughts:

2. How has God already shown His ability to bring beauty from difficult situations?

Your thoughts:

3. What areas of my life need me to release the ashes and accept His transformation?

Your thoughts:

4. Write down three ways God has turned challenges into blessings in your life.

Your thoughts:

SECTION THIRTEEN
FINALLY, MOVING ON...NEXT

Reflection

You have journeyed through purpose, healing, and transformation. You have shifted within, let go of the past, embraced rest, and stepped into obedience. Now, it is time to move forward boldly into the next chapter God has prepared for you.

Moving on does not mean forgetting your journey; it means carrying the lessons, strength, and victories forward while leaving behind what no longer serves you. It is about embracing the unknown with faith, courage, and expectation.

God's next season is waiting for you, full of promise, growth, and divine favor. Step confidently, knowing that every step you take aligns with His plan. Your story is still unfolding, and the best is yet to come.

Scripture Meditation

"Forget the former things; do not dwell on the past. See, I am doing a new thing! Now it springs up; do you not perceive it?"
— Isaiah 43:18-19 (NIV)

Affirmation

"I release the past, embrace the present, and move confidently into God's next plan for my life. The best is yet to come!"

Prayer Space

Father, thank You for guiding me through every season of my life. Help me to step boldly into the next chapter, trusting Your plan and walking in faith. Renew my strength, fill me with courage, and let every step reflect Your glory.
Amen.

Reflective Manifestation

1. What lessons will I be taking with me into the next season of life?

Your thoughts:

2. What fears or doubts do I need to release to move forward?

Your thoughts:

3. How can I intentionally embrace the opportunities God
    is presenting?

Your thoughts:

4. Write a vision statement or declaration for your next
    chapter.

Your thoughts:

CONCLUSION
MOVING FORWARD WITH PURPOSE

Encouragement:

Carry the lessons, the affirmations, and the truths of your journey with you. Trust that God has more in store, greater joy, greater peace, and greater opportunities. You are equipped, empowered, and ready.

Closing Prayer:

Heavenly Father, thank You for walking with me through every step of this journey. Help me to carry these lessons, this faith, and this courage into the next season of my life. May my life continue to reflect Your glory, and may I always walk confidently in Your purpose.
Amen.

Reflection:

You have traveled through seasons of growth, healing, and transformation. You have embraced purpose, released what no longer serves you, and stepped boldly into alignment with God's plan. Every word you have written, every prayer you have prayed, has prepared you for the next chapter.

Your thoughts:

FINAL THOUGHTS
MANIFESTATION

You have written, reflected, prayed, and declared God's promises over your life. Take a moment to celebrate how far you have come.

The journey is not over; it is only getting started. What you have learned here will guide your steps, strengthen your faith, and empower your purpose.

Your Turn:
Take a few moments to write your final reflections, prayers, or declarations for the next season:

Your thoughts:

NEXT STEPS

Thank you for using the *Journal: What God Has for Me is Mine: It Has My Name on It!*

I hope this journal has encouraged you, reminded you of your purpose, and inspired you to walk boldly into the blessings God has prepared just for you.

Remember: What God has for you is yours; It has your name on it!

To help you further, look for the accompanying eBook: *What God Has for Me Is Mine.* It is designed to guide your reflections, prayers, and declarations as you apply the lessons from this journal.

I'd love to hear from you! Share your thoughts, breakthroughs, or questions; your story might inspire someone else.

Email: thecoachingcreator@gmail.com
Website Coming Soon: www.thecoachingcreator.com

Keep moving in faith, trusting God's timing, and stepping fully into the life He has called you to. The best is still ahead!

With gratitude and encouragement,

Dr. Tonia Ann Walker